Terry Wilson lives in Adelaide, South Australia. He is the author of two earlier books published by Austin Macauley Publishers, *Fifty* and *Natural*.

I dedicate this selection to the people I came to know and the friendships that formed while we were living at Hocking Place in Adelaide, where this book was written.

Terry Wilson

FOX SPIRIT

AUSTIN MACAULEY PUBLISHERS™
LONDON · CAMBRIDGE · NEW YORK · SHARJAH

Copyright © Terry Wilson 2022

The right of Terry Wilson to be identified as author of this work has been asserted by the author in accordance with sections 77 and 78 of the Copyright, Designs and Patents Act 1988.

All rights reserved. No part of this publication may be reproduced, stored in a retrieval system, or transmitted in any form or by any means, electronic, mechanical, photocopying, recording, or otherwise, without the prior permission of the publishers.

Any person who commits any unauthorized act in relation to this publication may be liable to criminal prosecution and civil claims for damages.

A CIP catalogue record for this title is available from the British Library.

ISBN 9781398427594 (Paperback)
ISBN 9781398427600 (ePub e-book)

www.austinmacauley.com

First Published 2022
Austin Macauley Publishers Ltd®
1 Canada Square
Canary Wharf
London
E14 5AA

Fox Spirit

Walking past the building site
in limbo these last two years
waiting on the next pile of apartments
up to the flight paths
I noticed a house that had not been there before
rising on a small corner
of the vast block so devastated by building activity
a single storey residence
with well-established garden and trees
ornamental water a haven
behind a high wall which I couldn't see over or through
I had a good idea what lay behind
the type of garden etc
based on what houses are in general

how long since I've passed this way?
surely it was only last week
am I that unobservant or self-obsessed
that I never noticed it!
and how odd that approval was granted
to build a house right here
on a construction site
in the way of major money
how is it possible
I decided it was impossible

I knocked at the gate
as is my right as a local
the gate seemed solid enough
it gave a good loud knock
I heard footsteps approach
a Chinese woman opened it a few inches
her face elbowed over sideways to look through the gap
with the effect that her eyes were placed one above the other
I have read Chinese short stories and know
a thing or two about fox spirits
Are you a fox spirit? I asked her directly
Yes, I am, and this house is an apparition
You asked me this last week
How did you get out?
she said crossly

A Line is Drawn

A line is drawn in the higher atmosphere
Sharp and metal under the sun

With the wind up there, it soon wavers
And looks more like what it is, vapor
Coughed out of silent engines

I hear there's white lace
In the skies over
Every worthwhile city worldwide
More planes than ever, is that all it is?
Crossing and intersecting flight paths
Make a fine net for us
Viewing on the ground

And how are we to get to Mars now
With the Earth locked down!

Chair

A young lady is cracking up in the lane outside
I can see her grey and small in a white smock
On the door camera
Our only view and only in that direction
She throws a chair at
A man grey and tall and
Momently he falls over
Then gets up and throws it back
Only in our street will
There be a chair out there
Ready

Crashed

Back on earth down from the moon
The re-entry fried our controls
And we landed somewhere in the world
Somewhere else in the world than the aircraft carrier
And the martial music to lull us in
No bacterial swabs welcoming us home this time
Instead we the three of us are walking
With helmets dragging by a hose over our shoulders
But otherwise in full suit
Letting the senses explode
The air on the face
It is stiff and cold
Migratory birds are being blown into us
A whole row of them land on our space shoulders
For a rest
We are walking down a hill on a fire track
The fire happened here long ago
So it's shale and grey hills
We go down one side and up the rise
Clearly the middle of nowhere
We talk to each other on our intercoms
Every inch of the earth is full of life forms
Just like it was on the moon
We're just one example
Just three examples

Cellular soups
The Russians will have a field day if we are in Russia
Finally the helicopters come in
Thudding the sky
And we have our music and swabs

Garden

A stand of trees exists
somewhere out of Jericho
in the endless contemplative desert

Wherever you journey from
it is weeks of walking away

You could drive but
the roads give out
sand slops over them
or the car stops working

Where you start walking
is the journey
and it is weeks from that point

The map that shows this place
is tattooed on my back
where I have trouble seeing it
I have to walk backwards to see it

Of course one becomes delirious with thirst
imagining water and the water of life
to be the same thing
water you lift

that runs down your arms
and face

What does it look like, this orchard of the desert?
it is arid
the trees are cardboard
there is a tap
a tap hundreds of miles from anywhere

The water is sweet
not brackish
how can that be

Gardens

In fatherhood
his gentle hand
reached the tree down over us sitting there
to provide fruits of different types and shelter
the wood allowing him

When they came to write the story of his life
no one said he was foremost a gardener
and that gardening is the next step
make a tree and *the* garden will naturally follow

Everything he pruned off
here was the miracle!
grew back immediately in profusion
and flowers followed him with their faces
as he walked
because they loved him
we were less straightforward
and didn't think in the terms that flowers impose
in those days
when he was alive
but we liked how he thumped the ground
with the heft of his rake or spade
expounding his word
in the middle of digging a furrow

and look how crooked his borders are
it's a masterpiece of natural engineering
what he sought to teach us was the same
shambling and rambling
not at all precise as it is in the texts

Luck

Living in town
I walk everywhere
I go back streets and lanes for preference
seeking the hidden way, so to speak
now we *live* in a lane
the lane has a lane life
every step everywhere
reinforces a line of mind across a geography
which is me an extension of me
me when I am not here today
that is it will survive me
even then when I have not survived me
it is a vertical sort of walking
walking in town
crossing roads in a dream
the cars negatively geared towards
people not in machines
nevertheless like to avoid me and seem to like me
my eyes ratcheted up instead of down
going up a building
I live
death is not an option
death is an opinion
a Chinese monk selling a Guan Yin medallion
steps up to me and only me

and tells me I am very
lucky
to be thus approached
I actually believe that too
I lived here most of my life
and never see a face I know from all those years
I have lived here longer than friendship
and every face is my face on a stranger
we have all aged out of parallel
and we become unrecognizable
we have to tread over them
or thread through them
sometimes there they are on my very doorstep
drinking drop by drop
not wanting to be trouble
a voice that is hardly there anymore
but still happy to talk
the domicile doesn't look habited from the outside
once it was a factory and it closed down
it still has the original polished concrete floor throughout
pockmarked where the metal shelves once stood
though they see us going in and out through the blue front door
it still makes them jump when we turn up
some of them are friends now
our neighbours
neighbours who don't put down roots

Out and Free

we run with bell sounding footfalls on the earth
we flee forwards and know not to look back
and yet we look back
we are out we relent we look back
our will or purpose or is it just neck muscles
spasm
and we freeze still while deep down in miles of desert
miserable turning to water

the brief indulgence of remembering with our eyes
that old life that held all our loves
catch it as it goes
and we go with it

it all comes down with a cough of dust
which in turn is caught by the winds
and blesses the agricultural lands with a thick blanket
that blocks the sun
and we caught here like a dead tree
seeing that
for centuries
our eyes too wooden too wood to even close

Skin

Once you cross over the body
Close your eyes and wish
You can go anywhere
And look like anyone
And be anyone

But once past the child stage
And grown a beard and refusing to go out
This leaping up awake at the heart
Is oddly too free
Signposts are without end
Let alone the way they point to
After play
You want it to be different
So it is

The house you built up a mountain
And the wind picking up

Night Night

lay back and a tunnel appears
much too dark to be Death's
said to be a bright light
leaving the earth, you move along it

you are walking around the house
in your underwear
with a bucket and shovel
collecting cat poo

soak crisps in water or a sauce
and they will reconstitute to the
original potato or chicken or prawn
they came from

a smoke detector
is whistling like
a bird that needs
a new battery

books that are thrown into a pan
thicken on a low heat
the film of the book
bubbles on top

throughout the night
trucks drive by the house
creating a comforting sound
like rain

Sleep Not

floated on voices coming from
outside in the lashing forest
through that door
wore a mohair jumper
which was armor
imagined I was a prisoner
unable to lie down
let alone sleep

fish swam in and out of me
some of the fish were speaking some were talking
it was impossible to distinguish
my mouth was having its nightmare
about becoming wet and overflowing
but I was also underwater
impossible to distinguish

It was midsummer
And I was wearing a jumper

everywhere the world was awake

The Morning Star

Looked at the star too long
A pencil of light entered through his eyes
This is how people become black holes
The light cannot escape the gravity of the body
The clothing is sucked in through the pores
Then every physical object in the vicinity
Then the earth and the moon
And still he is hungry

St Paul in the City

Birds flew out from his every footstep
That's possible because he wore sandals
And not closed shoes
Once all the birds were gone
It was the time of angels
They walked step for step with Paul and
Wouldn't fly for him when he asked and
Knocked him with their staffs and berated him
He woke with sand filling his mouth
Staring direct into the sun
Seeing black-filled visions
They had beautiful words for that experience
And he wrote what they told him to write
He liked the birds more
Chatting and chuffing to him
Reprimanding and reproving
All in good nature
Between us, they never shut up
Whereas the angels were beyond-souls
Inopportune
Wait here until He comes
And love your lot
Carry Him on your back
Already giving up in his heart
He is in a room in a boarding house in a city he is lost in

He doesn't go out
People shout out in pain in the night
It is all perfectly wrong
And yet it stops from sleep
Then from behind and to the side and in front and from above
A hand touches his shoulder
He almost dies
So happy is he

Overhead

we stepped off the boat directly into the hold of the trees
up into the canopy of the trees we go
we never touched the ground
the trees will have ye
the branches are the roads here
wooden milking buckets are hung each quarter mile
to catch water
they bing bong into each other
as if we were at sea
this is the extent of the amenities available
for the hot traveller not used to vertical ways
above the bucket line
it is traditional to remove shoes and glasses
proceed just as we are
empty
go by feel and vague outlines all of green
suddenly you break through at the top
and breathe blue air again
and it is like a hat
tree loping elephants and striped crocodiles
full of funnels
are on us now
they slurry out of holes in the boles
and swallow us whole
swallow us often

it is what we love
you can't always be walking
they give us a ride
while we are inside
but it takes your beauty
one day you are a purple orange bloated face
hanging on with your lips
and no one wants to eat you
how sad that day

Run

come with me run
your feet once they settle once will take hold
and your legs walking against you
will stretch down
comfortable and sleepy in the ground
suddenly wood will rise up your body
look around you, this is a forest of human souls
that paused at this point
when a soul dies, an immortal soul
that is significant for all
so, let's go, don't stop

sick of food
I lived for a time on cups of tea
later I lived on sunlight
even that, that especially
left me feeling bloated and distended
we can limit what we eat
but there is no limit to the sun
unless you go inside, unless it's night-time, etc
even then he would suddenly appear
breaking the rules
pumping up the body to new extremes
I started drinking water again in that period

a few sips at first building up
in that way I started my long road back to health

Mammalian

Right now, everything feels safe
Please keep us rock free
Free like the rocks
Rocks tumble at odd times from up there
Birds bring them and drop them
We enjoy not being hit
It's fun to leap out of their way and
We the survivors at least have developed a proficiency
There used to be a mountain adjacent to our property
But the incessant rock fall has reduced it to
Almost nothing
It has gone flat
We no longer have to
Look above our shoulder all the time

I lay there
Feeling warmth and comfort and being surrounded
A typical mammal
The rock formation sits for hundreds of years
So solid you could build a hotel on it
And a cable car to it
Then dislodges because a cloud goes over
A rock shouldn't move
But startles itself

Care of Shoes, Care of Others

I come in from the wet parks
My shoes covered in clippings
How hair is, on the sides of a bald dome
It is up the sides of the shoes, a few strands on top.
I close the door to take my shoes off
Because it is very public where I live
I am always careful not to insult
A passerby on the street when
I reopen the door to brush off my shoes;
How contemptuous would that be,
Flicking the debris out into the street
Right where someone is standing!
Often there is an opportunity to sweep up
More generally outside,
Broken bottle glass, fast food cardboard
There are bins that seem to have
A permanent home there
Opposite our door
I am very happy for them

A Rag Picker

After almost a lifetime of being a unique human being
(On a tree there are no leaves entirely identical
though superficially some are similar
and hang in gangs)
one day just shy of death
when it was tantamount to too late
standing on the rubbish hill of your life
like a rag picker
hoping to breathe a fresh breeze again
hoping that a new gurgle of life will squeeze through
your tired back
you realized nothing and no one is unique
and how childlike that is
and any preferential treatment you might expect and demand
from the world
the world that loves you

About Face

we are close talkers
almost joined at the lip
it makes for best communication
not all the face fits into our view, we are close close
on you I see still
the rough of your cheek made of tarped over gorse
your mouth with its irrigation ditches
your eyes where animals come to drink

and occasionally brow leans on brow
making use of space more efficiently by
moving to no space
why complicate complicated things to say
by saying them at all
when we can lean brow to brow

and special moments when
faces disappear like sand into each other
and lumber into the month of dune
because we can't always be awake, stay awake

and who knows what passed between us
what was said
being so immediate
words that take time are out of earshot

the traffic between us is a deep deaf rumble
like traffic

City Sufism

The bin was not emptied
The truck did not come

I rang the council
This was Saturday morning
It's possible a truck might come out
On a Saturday

The bin was still out on the Sunday
It's unlikely they work on a Sunday
Turns out
They don't

Monday there are four other bins
In the street
A sign of hope
No truck though

During the night
The bin is knocked over
While it is still dark
I pick up the thousand things

One has to persist
Take it in

And that is the day
The truck will come

Wednesday morning
The sound of a truck reversing
Unreasonable joy wells
But it is the green bin truck

It is Wednesday still
Tonight, I will bring it in
It rules your life
Rubbish

Dutch

What if you were Dutch?
How would you be different?

You would have an accent
You would have had it all of your life
Not just from the moment of this question

You would have Dutch parents
The ones who gave you that accent
Perhaps you still visit them
Or live with them
They would be your biological father and mother
As far as anyone knows
As far as records show

The parents you knew before don't exist
They will feel a few weeks
Of strangeness
Without being able to explain why

You can live
Anywhere in the world
And still be Dutch
Where you live is not
Affected

So, continue to live here
With us

Flies

every fly in the world
will probably die before I die
so, what a big event it will be when I die
for flies

it is part of our mystery
that we have ladders of relationship leading everywhere
unknown and unconsidered
with so much built on it

I say every fly
but the exception might be
flies who live in the world's deserts
which is probably the majority of them
they may live for decades
because in a desert there are not many
predators that will eat flies
plus flies love the heat

Ancient Ant History

ants the great colonizers
journeyed to new continents
as people also did in a later era
ants went under the oceans
deep through the sands
digging their needle point tunnels
sometimes thousands of miles
sometimes they dug up
in the wrong places
and the sea came pouring in
the ones we know about of course
didn't do that
perhaps a very few
when they came out of the ground
it was air they gulped down
when all is dark and damp
ants carry a bubble of air
upon their antennae
and they suck on that
because they don't have mothers
ant historians say that ancient ants
floated on leaves to cross the oceans
it seems unlikely
thousands of miles even further in kilometres
in all weathers

perhaps it was in the hair of migrating beasts or hunters
they came
but the ants were there first
the tunnels are more or less true
a single ant decided to prove the theory
attached a fine fishing line to his thorax
to prove his expedition
followed the ancient tunnels
a rumour of former selves
the tackle wasn't long enough
it lay behind him blocking his return
after several years he came out
of a hole in Africa let's say
he wrote it all down

The New Earth

the earth appears in our sky
and all people gasp

it has retained its
bright blue lustre
across the years

either it was a dream dreamed
by the residue of humanity
that could still dream
that could still dream dreams
that could leave the earth

or it was a dream by
the earth itself, herself
the dream of the prisoner earth
a sort of cry

either way a dream out of the ground
and a wild hope

what is this new earth?
is it hurtling towards us to destroy us?
and destroy itself in the process?

that would make it a cannon ball
with the blue shapes painted on

The Results

If we are looking for water to sustain us
In the drystone places of the earth
A well is what we do
Once we puncture the stream
Surging through the rocks below
Miles below,
It surges up like oil does spuming,
The land is brought back to life from that foot rain
People move in with their cows and sheep
And eat it out and
In a generation there's no more generation
And it's back to desert again

Down deep in the spume hole
People are piling up!
Sometimes bodies come shooting up
When the water's on
People being very practical
Want to use the hole
They use it to jump in
They are struck with a bleak notion
How shallow their lives are
Next to the mysterium that
Has grown around this hole,
Said to be bottomless

It is called Measuring with the Body
As they disappear down down
If they are still conscious, they will be acutely awake,
And look up
They will see a star
The sky through the opening of the shaft so far from them
Is concentrating into a single event, called a star
It marks the moment life leaves the body
It hurts the eyes
To look at that bright star
And of course, it injures the star
To be looked at
To be seen like that

The earth is hollow like a gourd
A few meteorites have crashed through
And rattle around inside
Now the bodies of the jumpers 'land' in here
The meteorites once brought the germs of life
Now they see the results

Quarry Play

after forty years the original cast of
Peter Brook's production of The Mahabharata
what is left of them
decided to reprise this mountain of an undertaking
which takes a whole night to play out
and which is played in a quarry and not a theatre

Peter Brook is dead
Krishna is much weightier
and has really turned blue
Arjuna the great archer wears glasses
though just the frames no lenses
because he is still keeping to his disguise
after the year spent hiding in King Virata's court

is it a case of older and wiser?
the actors are less mobile now
unable to stand for long periods
and they turn that to a strength
they sit
it is what wisdom looks like
they sit in their ochre costumes against the cold
the whole action is them sitting
fast in meditation
the whole action is in them

here is an empty stage with them on it
they first walk ramshackle on
namaste the audience
and sit and that is it
in their heads in their foreheads in the spot between the eyebrows
they hold their attention
and visualize the scenes of action for us
for all of us for the world
replicating the method of composition of old Vyasa himself
never moving even their lips barely breathing
of course they are actors they are acting all this
sedentary is hard to do for twelve hours
they are great technicians but not perhaps great souls
not ultimate
separation still exists in the world with them in it
and they stand up at the end and receive applause

a young boy tells what is happening in their visualisations
reading from a text
that boy is older by the end
he is the grandson of the youth in the original production
the Bhagavad Gita is reported by royal Samjaya to the blind king
Dhritharashtra
so it was for us
nothing to see or look at
relying on another's words
hoping they are correct

an elephant wanders onto the stage unscripted
a gasp! Ganesh!
what have these characters conjured up!
no, just an elephant
unusual as that is
such is the magic that a western audience
could sincerely wonder if briefly

we begin to thin out in the dark
one by one
the war scenes are too late in the show
when the sun rises
musicians sit with the actors
sitars and zither and tabla
and play the new morning raga
soporiphic and beautiful
a weak dawn
the chorus of bird life waking up
only a few people have stayed the whole epic
a few laughing souls
happy whatever
in the presence of that Krishna
the only one they ever had
Lord Krishna who burned forests down
who said a lot more in the last production
and came again just to sit together this time
for these hours

Pond

The reflection in the water
Is not your face
You are startled to see
The face of a stranger

The reflection looks up
And the same thing happens
It doesn't recognize the face
And shimmers like electrocution

Or the reflection
Mimics your shock
But feels nothing inside
Has no inside

The Offending Radio

his radio was cranked up to full volume
playing songs of the sixties through to the eighties
walls of houses do the opposite of what you'd expect
they amplify the music that comes from outside
finally got the better of me
and I went out to shut him down
he was stretched out on the pavement
asleep the radio right by his ear
hand playing on the outsides of his pants
not a time to rouse him
half an hour later a police car pulled up
the radio switched off almost violently
I could hear through the walls
next extreme shouting and rage
because the radio was confiscated
the police car door slammed and
the car drove off in indecent haste
people who have very little
have even that taken
I heard him not long after
reporting his loss to a female voice
who must have been from a different squad car
apparently his recall was poor
because he said someone from the streets

had taken it
can they look out for it?

Sky Ladder

I was asked to hold a ladder steady
Whoever *that was* runs up it
And disappears into the sky

I couldn't see the top of the ladder
And I couldn't see him when he reached the top

I was caught here
If I draw back my hands now
The ladder will fall down
Leaving that man,
For it is a man this time,
Stranded up there

I can feel the weight of the sky
When I put my hands out
But now it's bound up with
The weight of the ladder
And the weight of that man
A weight on my hands
And a weight on my mind

Old Man

riding an ox backwards
only a lumbering ox is slow enough
for a journey where you never arrive

the mountains are wild and beautiful
how you ride to them
is a teaching for others
so, you are facing backwards
facing back
you are not thinking about
a good place
to set up camp for the night
it is where the ox stops

from the mountain perspective
your back means you are going away
it will take them some time being mountains
to realise that you are moving in the same direction
as the ox you are sitting on

plus, you look foolish

My Flat Hand

'The death of surrealism' came to my door selling vacuum cleaners
No, I need a piece of paper with an address written on it
Have you got one of those in your kit!
Even the corner of the piece of paper torn off
As long as the address is on that
I *have* a vacuum cleaner
Last time I used it it blew the piece of paper
Out of the window across the roofs
It was on blow function not suck function
Luckily there are many other addresses that will do
Perhaps you should try them

He who lives by the plate
Has a plate on his head
And a plate up his sleeve
These are resting positions for plates
He dropped and broke the third plate years ago

Like storks
They winced with every kiss
Until she caught his mouth in her mouth
And created some suction
Like a wading lake
I touch the surface with my

Flat hand
The water wobbles
As I go further under
My hand wobbles

Banging on a Door Once More

A woman is banging on a
Heavy metal door
Yelling her broken story to
Someone outside with her who loves her
I hear clapping and laughter and her
When everyone is shouting at the same volume
That is relatively speaking a conversation
A loud orchestral chord
Crashes into our air space
Every nerve in us is an instrument in that orchestra
And right now the strings are stretched
And the wood winds are chair legs
Recitative is over
The chair
A chair that walked here by itself
Under its own stream
Only for this!
There is a wrench-apart sound of tearing wood
With the leg she smites the metal door more to get in
She is very reasonable
We are human too
Just look at our faces
It requires you to open the door to do so
To open all doors
Though we may be laughing

We are crying
Look at our faces
Our faces serve us up like trays

Going Round

Going round in a straight line
You encircle heaven
Long into your journey toward home
Notice you resist arriving
Every house you called home
Is merely a shed to park your car in
These buildings were made of water
Sometimes of tears
And placed together in one long line
Formed the river
When these buildings seemed solid
Mortar rather than water
They were mighty comfortable
Suddenly they become unviable
The bed breaks, the fridge breaks
And you run out the door
Hair on end
Watching yourself in dismay
Every day started like that
Keep escalating behavior!
Then the water has you again
You sicken, here it is again
You hollow out
You are someone's boat
Hats are too far drawn down to recognize

Actually ride on you, what an escape!
Crash and scrape by tall outcrops of rock
Maiden chorus voices sing your slingshot journey
Hallucinations you can trust
What I heard underwater

Brothers and Sisters

People left the city as too clamorous and evil
And went to the desert
But people being people
Made a city in the desert
With tens of hundreds of recluses banding together
And resettling there
And yet there was no error in all this
No delusion
Suddenly a tide turned
And we were carried out

Yes, I am
Interested in
The Desert Fathers and Mothers
Most of all
They were
Brothers and sisters
Theirs, yours, mine

It happens in times of war
Very peaceable people
Most do not wish harm
Do the uncharacteristic thing
Decide en masse something that for the most part
Is already decided for them

People are not individuals ever

The sun feels sick
It looks pale and is running a temperature ha ha
In its sensational heat
As in sand forever without trees
Everything is flat and open
There is no single line
No single life
This is where we have to draw the line ourselves

It's All Hanging Out

How we hang a shirt to dry
Front facing out or back facing out
Tells us everything
Socks looking at each other
Or looking away
Each one dreaming of the foot

I accepted the laundry in fact wanted the informality of the laundry
As my room in my first house away from home
The laundry didn't have a door so I dressed in quick snatches
When the adjoining room the kitchen
Wasn't occupied
No one living there invested in the house
There was no furniture of our own
Emptiness wasn't a virtue or Buddhism

Another house I had a bedroom
Salt damp frothed the walls, it was covered by hessian
I lived in a sack
Though it was colorful hessian
The owner lived across the road
And collected the rent in person every fortnight
I suppose he was checking we weren't trashing the place
But how he could tell was unclear

He never fixed the broken window in the kitchen
It was small and high up, unassuming
All our personal books and music
Lived in our bedrooms
Like we were still living with our parents
Underwear – is it positioned behind the other clothing
Bigger clothing
So neighbours can't see it
Or doesn't it cross your mind?

Journey to the East

All along the forest trail
Naturalists sat sunning
Several miles of them
I had to step over legs and
In between legs
In my hiking boots

People who saw light
Found moths floating in it
There! a grey movement
Too sudden to see after
Which might have been the eye itself
Going grey

I could hear a flute up ahead
Off in the forest
There it is again, that flute
It was always ahead of me
One tree away
A turn of the path
The music went miles away from the trail
I had trouble finding my way out
Which is all I wanted by then

Return

By this time, time
Has reversed
We step into
The drip effect of
History
Events well known
But backwards
History was always
Just a series of
Woodblock prints
So we are looking at the
Same thing
From right to left
Rather than left to right

Lives Forever

In a dark rarely visited corner of the museum third floor
The caption on the glass display cabinet says
Lives forever
A grasshopper from the sub-cretaceous era
Still has movement
You have to be young to see it
a year on from the last event
he suddenly extends a leg
And scratches behind his ear
Afterwards you think did that just happen?
Did I really see that?
Children stand and watch for hours
Hoping this is the moment
It is like a slot machine
Will it pay off?
Nothing happens in endless time
It all happens right now
But nothing is happening right now
He is dry like a leaf that dropped off the tree
Sometimes he is found hanging upside down on his perch
He is helped upright by a gloved attendant
He is a million years old
no one is older than me
This dragonfly looks forward in time to us
That is our fate too

We live forever
Both the dull and the life of it
Skulls all in a row
Hammered with rubber mallets like a dulcimer
Make a satisfactory pock pock sound
When the teeth are nothing but fillings
Might even ring like a bell

Room

His room glows not just under the door but through the door
Neighbours complain about radioactivity and hydroponics
To them he is just an old man who lives in the back
The view from his window is blocked by the next building
Which you can reach which you can touch its rough face
The gap between buildings is filled with rubbish and rats
But this is Son of God who can see very well beyond brick escarpments
When he is interested in sky

He has been given notice but
He is digging in his heels
He is everything so he can be petulant
This is his room of many years
Instead of making his room a shrine
This was his desk this was his chair this was his typewriter
And having ecstatic singing queues up the stairs
As soon as he's out the building is demolished
Hard not to take it personally
Heaven help the other people living there
Who are rendered homeless

River Poem

When the river arrives at the ocean
the same river is just starting out thousands of miles away
there is a rush at the beginning
and rushes at the end
she thinks why hurry
when we arrive, we won't be a river anymore?
fish swimming upstream
coming home from their stint in the navy
bring news of what is to come
absorption into the Whole
the salty sea
But for now, lying in the sun and in the moon
our river is fat and drooling
home of the hippopotamus
she is a hippopotamus herself
in time she senses salt ahead
salt leaves a taste in the river mouth
she can't flee because she's not in flood
it's too late to run white and go wild
the land here is flat as flat
sand banks shaped like perplexed brows appear
the river is the last ditch between them
she sails on shaped by them but not stopped by them
a million wading birds sing her over

throats warbling with shells they couldn't pry open without
hands
the first tides she has known
rush up and rinse in
and boats of sail and a line
of oil tankers making a false horizon

The Most Living Thing

a leaf fell off the branch
the sky did not hold it
it was terrified like all life
but did not want to make a noise
it was picked up rubbish
it gripped that hand
the hand did not hold it

The Moon is Still Bright

He hides badly in the branches,
Then suddenly there he is
Rather jocular, rather funny
Perhaps there are cows on the moon
And he is wincing every time
They put a foot down
Or perhaps there are people on earth
Every time people on earth
Put a foot wrong, he is wincing
Whatever it is, I was overjoyed
(I don't want to say over the moon
But that's where this leads me)
I spent the next minute
Looking at him
I stopped for that long

Toy

a red scrap of a dress
thin legs one on each side
alone 8 o'clock cold go to bed
a student from overseas
still sad to be away
she has a violet light bulb on
in a culture where the light is white
here violet light means insect zapper
for her it is like a soft toy

Angel

Eyes like holes rather than souls
All the way through to the paper they are drawn on
Perhaps she looks directly at me
And yet doesn't know about me
The eyes of an angel
Are oddly black and uninhabited

Her glued-on wings have
Dropped from her shoulders to the middle of her back
What can be done?
We can only shrug like she must

See her feet there are none
She stands on the horn of her robe
Why have feet when
The rim of a circle meets your needs

Smile is a goldfish
And eyelashes are silver
Understandably she is delighted
For as she clasps her hands
A giant butterfly lands on her dress

Ants

Walking through flowers
Some heads will be crushed
Small creatures, ants and crap
That claim the path
Get walked on
Is there a quota of acceptable fatality?
Before liability kicks in
Karma kicks back?
It is the colonization of every square inch by footed animals
Without requisite care or supervision or responsibility

Death Across the Day

Last night I had a death dream
It was set in a high room
Up many steps
I had been there before at night
Or so I dreamed
But this was the first time
The only time (?)
I would climb them in day light

This evening at meditation
Our theme for the talk was
Life, Death and Impermanence
It is very modern of us, isn't it?
To believe in no survival?
There is no person in the person
And yet it is just the opposite
We are like
At an airport
All the planes are inhabited

As I am walking home in the dark
Along bright windows
Expecting it any moment
As if the dream and the discussion
Had appointed this day

I thought
Very curious, life
As if I'd already crossed over

Heart

We are divided in two
Then the fabric is torn into strips
The impossible sun
Another world
The world we came from
Puts us in his mouth and chews
But we are made of cotton
The sun can't get purchase
His teeth are too soft
He spits us out
We land as gob on the earth
And drape around the earth
And are the sky
The cloth skies

Humans are loud
In many cultures people
Shout as a normal
Mode of speech
They talk across vast distances
From one mountain to the next mountain
All night when sleep should be the project
We drape over the world
Our blue cloth

Eyes are drawn to the
Flower in the gutter
Rather than the drink container
Also lying in the gutter
Though the drink container is bright crimson
It's the flower we want to save
The drink container is not as important to us
Though it's more useful
But if we put the flower up somewhere out of the way
It will just deteriorate there
There's nowhere to go
And that's heart

Stone Homes

those men from the next valley
domesticated the wild sheep
and rode it into battle
they wielded sticks and branches
sharpened into points
wood has not survived the centuries
as well as tooth and bone and pots
and it hasn't given its name to an age
but it was a wood-based world
wooden hefting weapons were light work
to fashion in numbers
compared to stone
but they snapped too readily too
the heads of the vanquished often
proved too heavy
in their helmets

the exhausted families were driven away
into the hills and mountains
clans up there riding milking cows
waited in ambush
wooden buckets on ropes whirled in the air
making a whining whistling sound
which hurt the ears
the people of the plain

had never heard such a thing
there were a few cracked heads too
a settlement was established here
stone buildings are dated to this time
the pottery which spread throughout
the region in this period
is painted with agricultural motifs
reaping and sowing man and woman and child
scenes from below

then in the time it takes heaven to speak
which is many generations of earth
the king of the world
sent his envoy to call them back
to their garden homes on the plain
there is a white hole that must be filled
on his map of empire
it can only be filled with people
it is what they ached for
from up here they could see down there
a pulp of blue glaze far away
the land of our ancestors

The Stars

The stars we see
Are houses in the sky
With the lights on
Because there's no day
They leave them on all the time

People began leaving the earth
And arriving up there
As soon as people existed
There have always been those
Who walked with the gods

Nor is it hard to get there
We just need to alter our view of geography
Modern maps are the view from the sky
Ancient maps or no maps at all
The observer is on the ground

We can walk there
It is a long dusty trail but it can be done
There are way stations
To break our journey
To feed our animals

Tunnel Through the Trees

it is always still dark
when I go for these walks
where else go
if you are allied to the light
than dark places
I saw a star
through the trees black still in the greying sky
the star must have found
a tunnel of air
through all the wood
the same in me
a tunnel of air
I have narrowed down
to the size of the tunnel
and found a way of crawling along it
it is made of branches
not even intertwined
there are vast gaps
you fall out
I fell out
a number of times
it is not a tunnel at all!
my face and head and shoulders
ripped by spikes
emerged at the other end

always that same star
sat on my shoulder
moving in and out of sight
as I tipped and toppled

Trees Are Back

Trees are back for the season
hands full of green luggage.
Where did you go this year?
We went abroad to get warm
followed the birds
trees are more adventurous than is known
but happy to be home
there's nowhere like this little patch of earth
Look, right now the leaves are all shaking in soft air
soft hearted air
Seeing this, something corresponding to me replies,
My body is doing a dance too
not a dance anyone could see,
a shiver dance
if not a Shiva dance
The wind rises a little
and it's a knock about world
The nature you invariably meet or tangle with
is human nature
If something lovely is observed
that is you being a friend to you
It is spring and you are back and the trees are back
A bird accepts you
and arcs in the sky, where else?

And the sun glints on an insect, going gold
the tree showing it to perfection

The Calling Man

Sirens that stop suddenly here,
we have to smile; it happens so often.
Rubbish trucks beep in reversing
peeb peeb,
bottles breaking like silver on the street,
screaming rage in the police van,
public phone getting headed – who wins on that one!
Rasp of a decompressed door opening,
ambulance unloading or picking up.

And one only has to walk out
a city block in every direction
to be among peaceful armies of people
and peaceful places of parks and in trees
nature being calmer for all its fight to live
than human nature with all that happens.
A man has a friend on the fourth floor
he wants in, the night is cold, he missed the last tram.
And he shouts the friend's name for more than an hour.
The resident has been told on previous performance
not to buzz in people living rough to the block
else he'll be out to join them again.
A man of tough origins.
So, the shouting is left where it is, without response.
I'll leave, threatens the man at the gate, right I'm leaving now

but doesn't manage to.
Quietly at some point with everyone awake and electric
the other is secreted in and shut up.
I'll be evicted if you keep this up, his friend hisses.

why do we expect to sleep on nights like this
of which there is a collection?
What self-entitlement do we draw upon
when others less well employed
are inconvenient to our day?
Why should we get off lightly?
At what point are the police called?
What do we know about his life?
He doesn't know we exist and wouldn't care if he did.
All the people in their rooms within earshot don't exist.
If there was a siren now,
he would go around the block and come back and do it again.
He is not friendly.
So perhaps it is our place to be friendly, friendlier,
than him, than ourselves,
because we are the peripheral ones this time.

Walker

Sometimes, quite often in fact,
People I only know by the back of the head
Suddenly expire and lie on their
Backs in the middle of the
Road and let their arms
Dance full of sky
Under the influence of a drug
I want to say it is speed
For now, even the poem has overtaken me
In the last downhill mile
And just wants to make jokes

The Keys

the keys fell out of a pocket
everyone stood astonished
if they were seated they rose and
stood astonished everyone

it's not that the keys were special in any way
just car and house keys that we all have
yet for one out of time moment
(Out of time means it didn't end)
people everywhere
turned and looked
people here and far away
around the blind edge of the globe
what it was about
they didn't know
for that moment (Never ending)
they were in a dream or seizure
and obeyed its run
the earth stretched like a bird fanning its wings
enjoying the breeze after a hot spell
all of us thickheads
somehow intuited something was going on

Ah! Look!
around the world people everywhere

in unity and unison
are reaching into their pockets
and throwing their keys on the ground
to be astonished again
it is not as beautiful the second or the ten billionth time
eventually a little shamefaced
one by one they picked up the keys
forgot where he'd left them probably, she says to the family dog
and none of it ever happened

Path to Enlightenment

he moved into the forest
he was terrified of tigers and snakes
at night when it was pitch black
he sometimes strode back and forward
because he couldn't just sit with his terror
most of the time he stared out his fears
then in quick order he was eaten and bitten
he stared out that too but remained bitter
and carried it over to the next life

Buddha

1

Lying on his back in bed
He reached his hand back
And touched the wall
The house was his witness

Then he climbed the ladder
And touched the ceiling

2

Now he is old and fat
He brings a pot
When he collects alms
He dropped his bowl and broke it
Even though it was made of iron
The world is a broken place and
A place for broken things
The pot was given to him by King Bombisara
It is made of clay and brightly painted
People who feed these recluses day after day
Know the right amount to give
They give the amount that

Would fill an alms bowl
They have not accepted
This new lesson by the Buddha
That amounts can vary

The Living

There's a man passed out on his back on the road
He looks like he's looking at the stars
Though they wouldn't be visible
In the glare of the streetlights

A couple of brothers lift him out of harm's way
Their voices sound like ambulance personnel
But it turns out they're not

A stream of liquid comes out of him on his back
Like ripe fruit
He could die
The living are going over to look
To lend their expertise

Arrow

the meritorious one
who once shot an arrow into his future
has in these last days
reached a place where that arrow will arrive
he tended upwards in life
he tended The Garden upwards
it was a jagged nervous-like track he took
but it was higher at the end
and with hindsight, the virtue of hindsight
his was continuous, a bright line
in the bright light

as he was settling in to the hospital cot straight after being born
(Not for long, don't get comfortable)
he was recounting to himself like multiplication tables
the list of all the previous mothers he has had
and this one the only one who matters now
who's she?
what this new name for the list?

the clouds moving across the sky and going behind the tree
his grandfather said that's us moving, the earth moving
not the clouds
partly true

Five Dollars

There are many shaven headed men
But they are not bald like a monk

He appears at my elbow
Out of the tapestry of crowded places

A transaction private and still
Occurs right there in the movement

He writes my contribution in pencil
In his book of ruled pages

It is done slowly
In a big childish script

Then he lowers his head
And bows back into the torsos

Food Van

In the alley at sunset
The sun makes a sword of light
On the security monitor
For half an hour the system is
incapacitated by light
you can barely see people there
they are even more like ghosts
or the ambulance parked
just the rasp of its doors
a whole ambulance or police car
is lost to viewer

Grab a handful of flesh
At the back of the neck
The face is pulled back and tight
Like a sock
All the soft areas
The eye lids, mouth, nostrils
go hard
a face that looks like a human house
no one looking out the windows
who would not want that?

Then He Was Released

some nasty little things happen on the road
between here and there
they fed him nothing but
metal filings, flakes of aluminium, fishing sinkers
while he was in gaol
he put on a lot of weight
after he came out
found they could trace his movements
he rattled with surveillance
mod gen's take on the ankle bracelet
now when he pukes
he cracks the bowl
heavy as

Lucky I have metal teeth, he thought ruefully
He was referring to the mouthful of fillings
he received as a child and young adult

he prayed to angels who wield a sword
please feed me keep me saved
he pushed the plate away
all the way across the floor
from now on he was not accepting food
food was going to kill him
two guards came in

wearing hardened gloves
forced his mouth open
and pushed the food in
with thick fingers

White

A white tree stands out in a white background
Overwhelming is the late afternoon sun
Shining in a line with our faces
I see people I know, or rather don't see
They step out of the sky
Miffed that I made them ghostly
It's the glasses, I excuse myself
I can hardly see a thing
I continue to live in a dark forest
There I cannot see myself any longer
Others exist better

Tip

once I was sitting right
the instruction was
breathe
breathe
breathe
I found I could do this
now do that 2 hours every day
later it will be 4 hours
2 in the morning 2 at night
he can read my levels
and knows it's not worth wasting his time
at home I didn't last
more than 20 minutes
it was excruciatingly slow
many peek experiences
at my watch

sitting just still
we can be almost geological
sit like a mountain it says in the guidelines
the streams that live on every mountain
are flowing upward
up the arms the shoulders the face
accumulate in a vast lake
a washed out blue

eventually the weight of water is too much
and the whole affair tips over onto its head
its feet jutting into the air
startling about for ground
and the streams start again to go to below
'Do not use words
there is only the one word'
'What word is that?'
'Find it'
'Is it cat?'
'no'

Water

The sound of the sea
The surge of the sea
Is a constant
In my skull
There is only water in there
The holes at my ears
Keep it in
We know ears only go in
Only go one way
Growing up I spent
Every day out in the water
I still hear my youth

Things We Talked About

somewhere on the continent of South America
is a big button
hard to press because it is the size of a house
it is the flush for the world's oceans
see all this blue on the map:
all of this water with its poo is flushed away
and replaced with clear clean water
inevitably many lives are lost
it's start again for everything

a footprint is left in the rock
the signature of a great teacher and magician
who once passed through these mountains
and turned the resident demons towards benevolence
(It fills with water
mosquitos breed in it)
knowing the structure of the foot
a body bone structure can be modelled
and the musculature
from that the face

The Man of Light

when the man made of light
trips on the stairs
he doesn't hurt himself
but rather blesses the house all the more
with his light splatter

when the man made of light
enters the house
the fresh refreshing breeze
which he seems to have about him
wherever he goes
means we can keep the house in lockdown
we don't need an open window
he is enough
we can breathe

when he smiles or otherwise shows his teeth
you can see your face
reflected a dozen times over
(He has more than the usual number)

because his is not a temporal light
there are no shadows
even on the inside
an X-ray if taken shows no dark details

not a clutch of bones nor notch of joints
leading to the question
what is he made of
shark sinew?

once a man made of light comes here
that's it for darkness
there's not even a night sky
added to that
there is no longer sleep
we are not tired

At First

at first love was
just that one word
Yes

then it began counting
the number of
Yeses

it could feel the turn
of Face
to Faces

though there was
only this one face

Back

Where are we going?
A curtain of trees flies open
In a startling way

Our trouble was we
Began past the body
We had to retrace our steps,
And lose our special sight
So simple and obvious
Once you once see it

Love was to be unpicked
We sent backwards the love as well
Once we could say love was all
But now we could only say it

Arriving at the body
We had to fall backwards to re-enter it
It didn't feel like it was even there
Though it must be
For we have stopped falling.

Bench

A long narrow path
Faded mildew bricks through the beds
Went to a bench at the far end
Diminished by the long stretch

By the time I get to it
All of a minute away, so a distance
In the intuition of the moment
Someone would arrive
Inside that minute sit there
Be expecting me somehow

A fateful feel in the air
As if all the trees had opened a curtain
For me to enter here
And were crowding to see
But strangulating the circumstances and
Possibly negating any chances

I've been watching you all your life
Now a meeting can take place
This confederacy of the bench

But I got there first
And it was I who had the proposed meeting on my lips

There were people around
But not the one I meant

Flounces

Faces joined at the kiss
Come away flat as pans
It's only after many years together
That faces grow back
Each gives the other some detail or other
Facial topography is exchanged and mixed
They dress alike as well
The same black colors and flounces

Tears are dropping upwards
And streaming in the sky
Our tears are leaving us
Abandoning us
Whales leaving the water
Here the language
'Dropping upwards'
Does not work anymore

Sole

If you watch the sole of your foot
How it is cold
And the shape of that cold
And that it doesn't have
Any height
You start to exist

In a Cemetery

Invader light fills the field where I was
Minutes ago
Some birds born to it, born to here
Will fall victim to it, to here
Their heads down grazing, biting water
Suddenly it was over them
Under the darkness of trees in time
I saw a huddle of mourning souls
People who sip life from the bottle on the streets
They were genuinely crying
Mourning the loss of one of their own
A circle of thick coats
One of the family is gone

Jubilation

people start by leaving
they have a map
but it was printed in the last century
on a loom

infinite sadness, the spiritual fact
is in every life
who has not lain down and cried?

it is all creatures
what is distinctly defining human
extends to all creatures
a bird in play
is just distracting itself

the narrowing path gets narrower
neuroplasticity affects everything but our brain
the landscape is a trampoline
no bigger than a trampoline either
once we step foot there and bounce
so does it

of course we have houses that
don't burn down all the time
and shopping is good

the pleasure crowd crams the streets
looking for people to be in
jubilant and jubilation

Making Us Ill

Suddenly people were setting fire to their cars
And continuing the journey on foot
We laughed with rancor
At the enormity of what we had just done
A corner had been turned
On any given night there were
Thousands of vehicles becoming tragic small suns
Or a late flare up of love

Time is making us ill
Its direction is down
Nothing has happened in our world
There is the slow creep towards extinction, that's all
After extinction what is there?
The earth

When I breathe out I'm gone
I breathe myself out
My lungs are the black lines of a tree
A tree standing in the snow
People under bright lights
Living outside at night
Vomit bile
Orange and green
Time is making us ill

The birds have expired
Their beaks lie open
As if saying something to silence
In the language of silence

Mindfulness

This morning I did my practice
I went deeper than ever before
It was like I was relaxed in a still ocean
Under the march of the waves
It was a womb moment
I wondered what the next layer
Deeper was
That was my thinking coming back 'what next?'
Or perhaps the voice was a kindred soul
Whispering to me
Helping me to steer the submerged boat
I expected to rise to the surface
Suddenly a hand grabbed my ankle
And pulled me into a void
I would never return from
The practice is to observe the feelings that arise

Bigger Picture

Let us make friends with friends
And death with death
The stream doesn't flow
Except back on itself
A rock that is outside the circumference
Of the wheel
Seems to jut out of nowhere
From outside the universe
And knock it off course
So it careens
We do not know the bigger picture
And notice none of this

Cloud

every cell in my body evaporates over a few years
and becomes part of the cloud around me
like a planet I have an atmosphere
when the planet has had enough and is close to death
it will be all atmosphere like Jupiter
my eyesight deteriorates over the years because
I am looking through more and more clouds

Lighthouse

on top of the world stands a lighthouse
light does not stand on a pedestal
it shines all the way to the ground
through every window and doorway
where the top of the world is located
is like trying to say where in the body we are
but this lighthouse was a built building
on a headland of cliffs over a wet region of the sea
in the time of human habitation
the lighthouse is a job to do
an arm reaching across a human view of water
once it was lighter and further
and sat more gently on the rock
but the keepers who would live in a place like this
so away from themselves
favoured a firmer stamp on the face of the earth
in time a living thing dies
the white shape crumples like a face
a face that could be smiling
it leans over to look at its feet
never knew it had feet, footings yes
by then the strong useful beams are looking the wrong way
down and up
to serve any purpose except metaphysical
perhaps it is a reassertion of true function

ships still don't crash
everything is all right in that respect
sheep have always come to graze here
there was always shelter from the brisk wind
by the building
now they are knocked off their feet
and lie on their sides and bleat
and the lord has to come out more often

New Start

I stand up out of my body
I walk along a darkened corridor
Atoms of wind with the impact of soft birds
Splash onto my face
Dust builds on my eyes
As if windows were taken from the house
Water stretches out before me
Calm and breathing
I sit in the shallows and get wet
This is the beginning of water
And a fresh start for me
Behind every door
Families are listening to the corridor
They sense something is different
They wouldn't know I am there
I make no sound they can hear

Old Path Many Years

These dry old paths
You can go for weeks
Without seeing a soul
Yet here is a figure
Walking towards me
It is the Lord
Every encounter is the Lord
But this really is He
I stood and roared with laughter
He approaching also stopped
When he knew me
And bent with laughter too
The path is old
But let us be clear
We still have some life in us
Look at us capering around

On the Screen Door

On the screen door
Every second intersection of the frame
Has a round rivet
To secure the metal mesh

These rivets
Are points of attention
And the metal mesh seems to extend
Out in circles from them

Although this is a trick of the affections
The gravity of the rivets is insignificant
And is not shaping the mesh in any way
Even with a screen door
Something so secular
You want something to be going on

Participant in Events

he is touched on the shoulder
by the bright and shining
and he says yes
it is a sudden blow
the body is thrown back into a wall
he rolls in agony rolling in sobs
screaming and begging remove it
while it is theologically inexact
the holy one really is a ghost at this stage
reaching out his hands
reaching in with his burning eyes
all that was bodily has gone to this man on the floor
all that was afraid and lost and betrayed gone to this man
it is the weight of the planet
with all that the man who takes the pain is righteous
and gazes up sometimes from the dust of the ground
out of his head perhaps
in shepherd adoration

later when it's still the same sharp hurt persisting
because it can't resolve if it must work
he will become bleak and bitter
there are many centuries that start from here
taking the world of man in that direction
but not now

with the sparkling lord around him
all arms

he was taken by the followers to a room
and held there
essentially a prisoner
they didn't know what to do with him
he refused food and stank and shouted day and night
of course pain wasn't unusual in those times
and didn't draw notice from the street
for his part, he was terrified of them
he couldn't understand their language
they were hooded and fanatical

Pass Out

in the street someone kicks a bottle
just to break it
usually breaks
this time it won't
it rolls triumphantly along
the next day it is picked up
and put in recycling and safety

the rain falls high up
and has already evaporated
before reaching the ground
lord you taught us to wait
yet it is happening hundreds of impacts
every second it is happening now
you also don't quite reach
all the way to the ground
full of promise
it doesn't eventuate

he howls and roars and scares
landlocked legs filled with sea
it is the women who talk him through
when he lost it they kept him safe
then he is off
limp walking around the corner

to comment loudly there too
really is stupid with drink
the women keep on steering him with their voices
they must be tired of it
and truth be told want to pass out
as effectively as he has managed
can't

Stains

the streets are a map of piss stains
kidney shapes with a runoff
like a string on a balloon
not welcome in someone's hand
never held aloft
these are like cloud shadows
caught in tarmac
the liquid underpinnings of
people massed together in thick proximity
eve to eve

when I was a child
the smell was of cats
today it's human
cats have the little faces
of baby humans gazing out of bonnets
their reputation as far as the pissing is concerned
was bound to be rehabilitated

Swell

The earth herself has an upward urge
An urge but not an urgency
It is really too flat and round
To get anywhere fast

And yet it is a magnificent achievement
That it has spread so far sideways
We never reach an end of
Her swift trancing dress swell
Beaches slide out of the water
For the first time ever, after that always

Town

He comes from a dry community and has just
Arrived in town to drink
That's my wife up there
She is about a block away walking on the road
That one's my niece
She is up further also on the road
He doesn't know his way around
He asks where the bottle shops are
We're having a good time tonight
Have you got anywhere to stay?
I feel careful on his behalf
Proprietorship of being one of the locals
I'm with my aunt at her place
Where are you from?
He said a place I didn't know and didn't retain
Red dirt Stuart Highway

After
There's twenty or thirty voices having a riot
The police car is parked there
Don't resist he says
Taking a man to the ambulance
Men are falling over while women shout at them
Shouting sense into them
It's freezing and one of the shouting men

Has thrown away his shirt
Thrown it onto a roof
Or at a car

Twilight

I am being taught how to walk the twilight way

Leaves let dropped on the sidewalk are the pen strokes of
A twilight language and system of writing

It is a highly personal communication because
It may exist only the minutes I am here
Already a wind is getting up behind me

I can't read leaf

It is Babylonian to me
Chloroform script
Before typing pools had typewriters
These are the dents clacked in soft clay by long nails
Lines and lines of crescents and smiles;
Instruction in dream stepping

What you do is walk it
Nothing is random
Some bits of tree laid at right angles bar entry
And must be opened like a gate
Others afford a clear on-way
Proceed with carelessness

Be relaxed to the point
Of receiving everything
And there is nothing to receive

Common Property

After a while talking loudly and laughing a lot
Thumping started on the door
At which I spoke through the wood
Pertly as one who can rely upon a house
To them who can't
'Stop hitting our house'
"Is mother at home?"
'Mother doesn't live here'
Confusion on the other side taking in that new information.
Slowly it became sad
An hour on there was moaning then a long howl
In the morning glass to sweep up
No need to throw water at it
Nothing wet to make wetter
I am amused at my fastidiousness after
So long living with the rubbish
After all, why not use our wall to lean on,
The outside of it is common property
Later they were taken off to a bed somewhere,
Drinks patrol
May they be happy

Fields

in traditional times
when the unnecessary was king
farmers ploughed their field not only along its length
but after they'd finished that taking the whole day
next day they ploughed *across* their field along its breadth
the first ploughing was just to get the ground wet so to speak
before the second ploughing could be accomplished
this is like the first and second pouring of tea in China
where the first pouring is usually discarded or bitter
naturally the first plough lines were churned under
the second plough lines
for some reason this seemed to worry the farmers
once it was gone they couldn't be sure a ploughing the length
of the field
had occurred
so they ploughed the length of the field again just to be sure
but the plough lines *across* the field were lost then
they were the second pouring so they had to have those
so that was done again
then someone asked where the lengthways furrows had gone
again
perhaps it was an innocent question
someone who *did* remember should have had a quiet word at
that point

Fictional War

years into a fictional war
we found each other
from the old life
you sat in a blanket
gripped closed

she smiled broadly despite a lot of bad luck
your front teeth are still intact I said absurdly happy
that's the main thing
during the artillery barrage that accompanied these fine words
the zooming in the air and the birdsong of bullets
even the wind
didn't buffet you
I suppose I was the same
we turned edge on like flight feathers
and it went right past us
although we were whispering in the scream and the roar
we were loud enough

Flowers

I recognised him by his history face
men rarely look up
they find the ground interesting
one day as long as night they will be in the ground
their faces covered in white cloth or in darkness
he on the other hand
his was caught looking by a cloud
I followed him watching his walk
how his ankles breathed into the earth
like a bellows
I remained back keeping distance with him
is this what it means to be a follower?
the road turned around walls and
veered him out of view
I hurried to catch up the corner
and he was standing there
a dark figure now
waiting for me
one can only laugh in such moments
don't stare at me in your hypnotising way
how great are thou
if you resort to hypnotism
as the seat of power?
then he laughed all electricity

his gaze lifted out of that cloud
and it was all flowers

Eyes in the Dark

the same glowing eyes everyone
has in the dark sometimes
reaching down and pulling off another
bite of railway track
like birthday cake
the train wasn't invented that didn't
hoot on your happy birthday
old blind men
bend over
first about a quarter
then deeper, a half
then able to touch the ground
with their yellow fingers
to pick something I can't see up
and just as slowly
go back through the clock
with the aid of a stick

Clamp

The postal van on its run to the outlying towns
Driving round a mountain
Knocks down a sheep on the road
Runs it all the way over bump-a-bump
Then stops to look back for the carcass
And it's gone, a bit of blood that's all
They have to pull the van to bits because the sheep
Has crawled up into the innards of the vehicle
And found somewhere warm
To nurse itself
Then a warm love lifts it, clamps it with big hands
Come home

Carried

What if everyone carried everyone else
We'd all be six inches off the ground
Here is the paper ground
Your name all over it
The shadows of your feet six inches above the ground
Mysteriously spell out an alphabet
Lifting and rolling as the paper convulses and convalesces
Like the small intestine
Everything is running, the feet, the ink, the
Leaves

Gang up of everybody against the one
And you get carried along by the armpits
By vast numbers of laughter
They ink the underside of your tongue
With high respect
You spit out shapes that are taken to be prophetic
They ink the bottom of your feet
And run you along the ground
You fill the field with your running
Leaving the paper traces behind you
With hard to say words
Mysteriously spelled out spells
In black and red

Then you see her up the front once
Like an audience surging on their bellies onto a stage
You take the first step of a long-ragged path
Loving but losing
Lecherous and grubby and totally inappropriate
For this new world, this new life experience
Large rays of the sun dazzled my eyes
Dawn stayed in one place
So I could see it
But as I said it dazzled me
Her name was Dawn I mean
There are a thousand small tracks
Where water has run
Patterns of snow melt
Where animals have come through
Going up to pasture
But which way is up?

Lemon

Squeezing a lemon out from its juice
When you drink it
It is solid
It gets caught in your throat
Causing a panic in you
Cough vigorously to clear your throat
It bounces up and down like laughter
Finally it lands
And will hurt your guts for a few hours

You will notice that few words
Have internal alphabetical order
And some lines are longer than others
That's being wave-like

Talking to the daughter who owns the music shop
Passing on a message to her father
Her mouth went into an 'o'
Like the sound hole of one of the instruments and
Her face became wooden
Maybe she was just listening well
And as if a string was plucked behind us
Immediately her mobile phone was out
And she was texting him
A tune we could hum

Leaves

A man was filled with leaves
He lived where the branches were blasted and black
No leaves grew on the trees anymore
He wanted to preserve the moment before everything changed
And leaves are the link that gives us birds in trees
And bird song and air fit to breathe
He filled his pockets with them and his hands held what they
Could hold
But it was impracticable
The pockets ripped
The hands dropped them to catch a ball
The leaves sat on a shelf inside his body
While all this was being worked out
And one day he found that this was his answer all along
He added more leaves and more till he was rounded out
And how unexpectedly human face those leaves were
As they got moved and manipulated by facial muscles
And rubbing thumbs
The subterranean grimace reaches the light as a smile
To look at him he looked like anyone else
But he was not
Because he was full of leaves
He was a little rough faced
Because the leaves were not even
But all people at that time were rough faced

And no one else had a good reason like leaves
It was a craggy time all round

Lake Poem

I won I won I won I won
shouts the man who won
very happy and very unhappy
tonight, despite the win
he will be bedding down in the street
perhaps he won at marbles at school
and in that he topped his class

Untidy bundles of clothes
are left everywhere
the human beings wearing them
have dissolved or drained off into the bitumen
and the clothes just fall
where they are standing
these clothes sometimes like their possessors
before them
get honked by cars
to get out of the way
the clothes without people in them
groggily comply and slowly stand up and
go closer to the wall
it doesn't auger well for the people side of the equation
who have given them their shape and their size
after that become unnecessary

there is a big hole in the mattress
which we have to sleep around
it fills with cold water from the ground
and becomes a small lake
it is a nightmare really
all night is feverish the panic not to roll into it
our bodies never lie straight
and during the day ache

It is something, a thing
it has grown to full size in a minute
a minute ago, it wasn't there
is it you?
that wet scrawny leggy big eyed
unhuman (but lovable in the same way)
newborn
just out of the egg
communicating in chirps and cheeps

Do you exist in the space
one inch above your head?
where do you stop?
imagine standing in that space
all of you fits in that inch
what are you standing on?
it's not your head
your head has come with you

Words are Finished for Good

1

There are things that stand still
enough to be seen
a face you have talked to for many years
for the first and perhaps only time
looks into yours
it is flat on
a face fluid and mobile in its joints in its segments
settles by a number of sloshes into a lake

Millions of bulldozers splash in on their annual migration
beeping and rumbling and mating
getting bogged getting towed
and they can't help themselves, they tidy it up
take out the reeds build some roads
move sand and make a beach
the face I started with
steps out of surprise
the geranium lips emerging from the casement of skin
and takes shape

2

Beyond words
the sheafs of writings held so dear
yet stacked in a leaning pile
leaning on the bookcase
wanting to be let in,
it's not that they are erased in that moment
but they never existed seemingly

3

A white chalk line in the sky
crosses a line of black crayon
that is the eye looking at itself
it cannot see the other eye
its brother
because the bridge of the nose rises between
so it looks at itself
this is the birth of consciousness